Turning Points in History

BROWN V. BOARD OF EDUCATION

Brienna Rossiter

WWW.APEXEDITIONS.COM

Copyright © 2025 by Apex Editions, Mendota Heights, MN 55120. All rights reserved. No part of this book may be reproduced or utilized in any form or by any means without written permission from the publisher.

Apex is distributed by North Star Editions:
sales@northstareditions.com | 888-417-0195

Produced for Apex by Red Line Editorial.

Photographs ©: AP Images, cover, 1, 46–47; Carl Iwasaki/The Chronicle Collection/Getty Images, 4–5, 6–7; McPherson & Oliver/Library of Congress, 8–9; Collection of the Smithsonian National Museum of African American History and Culture, 10–11, 42–43 (left), 43 (right); Heritage Art/Heritage Images/Hulton Archive/Getty Images, 12–13; Russell Lee/Library of Congress, 14–15; Library of Congress, 16–17, 29; C. M. Battey/Library of Congress, 18–19; Bettmann/Getty Images, 20–21, 22–23, 34–35, 36–37, 44–45; Library of Congress/VCG/Corbis Historical/Getty Images, 24–25; Shutterstock Images, 26–27, 32–33, 39, 48–49, 58; Lou Krasky/AP Images, 30–31; Warren K. Leffler/Library of Congress, 40–41; Rowland Scherman/National Archives, 50–51; Will Counts/Arkansas Democrat-Gazette/AP Images, 52–53; Lawrence Jackson/The White House, 54–55; Sue Ogrocki/AP Images, 56–57

Library of Congress Control Number: 2024942379

ISBN
979-8-89250-462-1 (hardcover)
979-8-89250-478-2 (paperback)
979-8-89250-508-6 (ebook pdf)
979-8-89250-494-2 (hosted ebook)

Printed in the United States of America
Mankato, MN
012025

NOTE TO PARENTS AND EDUCATORS

Apex books are designed to build literacy skills in striving readers. Exciting, high-interest content attracts and holds readers' attention. The text is carefully leveled to allow students to achieve success quickly.

TABLE OF CONTENTS

Chapter 1
SCHOOL STRUGGLES 4

Chapter 2
UNEQUAL ACCESS 8

Chapter 3
SUING FOR SCHOOLING 18

Story Spotlight
THURGOOD MARSHALL 28

Chapter 4
COMBINING CASES 31

Story Spotlight
BARBARA ROSE JOHNS 38

Chapter 5
THE SUPREME COURT 40

Chapter 6
LEGACY 48

TIMELINE • 59
COMPREHENSION QUESTIONS • 60
GLOSSARY • 62
TO LEARN MORE • 63
ABOUT THE AUTHOR • 63
INDEX • 64

Chapter 1

SCHOOL STRUGGLES

In 1950, Oliver Brown tried to enroll his daughter in school. Her name was Linda. She was seven years old. The Browns lived in Topeka, Kansas. Sumner Elementary School was just a few blocks from their house. But the school wouldn't let Linda attend.

Linda Brown (left) stands outside her home with her mother, Leola; her father, Oliver; and her sister, Terry Lynn.

Several of the students and parents who sued Topeka's school board pose for a picture.

Linda and her family were Black. Only white students could go to Sumner. So, Linda had to go to a faraway all-Black school.

Mr. Brown sued the school board. So did 12 other Black families. Their children had been turned down by white schools, too. The case was *Brown v. Board of Education*. It reached the Supreme Court.

SEGREGATION

Kansas was one of many states that segregated schools. This practice began in the 1800s. And schools weren't the only places that were segregated. States passed many laws that kept Black and white people apart. They went to separate stores and restaurants. They rode in different parts of trains and buses.

Chapter 2

UNEQUAL ACCESS

For many years, the United States allowed slavery. White people enslaved millions of Black people. Black people were forced to work without pay. They couldn't vote. They couldn't go to school. And they often faced terrible violence. Slavery ended after the US Civil War (1861–1865).

The conditions of slavery were awful. Many Black people tried to escape.

Many Black people became lawmakers after the Civil War. Hiram Revels (top left) was the first Black senator.

Lawmakers tried to help Black people after the war. They changed the US Constitution. Lawmakers added three amendments. These gave Black Americans equal rights. So did several other laws. The Civil Rights Act of 1875 was one. It banned segregation in public places.

NEW AMENDMENTS

In 1865, lawmakers added the Thirteenth Amendment to the Constitution. It ended slavery, except as punishment for crimes. The Fourteenth Amendment was added in 1868. It said all people born in the United States were citizens. All citizens had equal rights. The Fifteenth Amendment was added in 1870. It gave Black men the right to vote.

After the Civil War, Black people were often forced to become sharecroppers. This work trapped people in lives similar to slavery.

However, many white Americans did not want Black Americans to be free. By the 1880s, many of the laws and protections had been weakened. Courts ended some. And states passed laws to keep Black and white people apart. These laws were called Jim Crow laws. Segregation became common. And violence kept it going.

RECONSTRUCTION

Reconstruction took place after the Civil War. This period lasted from 1865 to 1877. During this time, the US government tried to help Black Americans. Soldiers tried to keep Black Americans safe. Laws helped people vote and attend school.

Activists worked against segregation. They tried to show the system was wrong. To do this, they often broke Jim Crow laws. Homer Plessy was one example. Plessy lived in Louisiana. In 1892, he rode a train car for white people. But he was part Black. So, police arrested him.

In response, Plessy sued. The case was called *Plessy v. Ferguson*. Plessy's lawyer said the arrest was wrong. He said having separate train cars went against Plessy's rights.

Signs often enforced segregated spaces.

The court disagreed with Plessy. So, he appealed. A second court disagreed, too. In 1896, the case went to the Supreme Court. It also ruled against Plessy. The court allowed segregation as long as separate spaces were equal. This case set a precedent. Many laws and cases became based on it.

A DIFFERENT VIEW

One Supreme Court justice disagreed. Justice John Marshall Harlan opposed segregation. He said it limited Black people's freedom. It also treated them as less than other people. He pointed to the Thirteenth and Fourteenth Amendments. They said all citizens were free and equal.

Justice Harlan (bottom center) wrote his own opinion separate from the other justices in *Plessy v. Ferguson.*

Chapter 3
SUING FOR SCHOOLING

In the 1900s, activists continued to challenge Jim Crow laws. Many were part of the National Association for the Advancement of Colored People (NAACP). This group called for equal rights for Black Americans. The NAACP often used court cases to make change. Several cases focused on education.

W. E. B. Du Bois was an early leader of the NAACP.

In 1938, Lloyd Gaines won his lawsuit against a law school in Missouri. However, he went missing a few months later.

Two important cases took place in the 1930s. The NAACP won both. Black students had applied to all-white law schools. The schools rejected them. Then the students sued. They argued the schools should let them attend. Courts agreed. They based this ruling on the *Plessy* case. They said there weren't any equal all-Black schools.

Black students study in a crowded, one-room school in Georgia.

In the 1940s, the NAACP turned to public schools. Segregated schools were supposed to be equal. But most were not. All-Black schools often got much less money. Buildings tended to be old. Classrooms were often crowded. Many lacked basic supplies. They didn't have enough desks or books.

UNEQUAL FUNDING

South Carolina had segregated public schools. In the 1940s, the state's schools spent about $221 for each white student. White schools had buses and libraries. They had separate classes for each grade. Meanwhile, schools spent only $45 per Black student. Many Black schools had just one room. Most didn't have running water.

The NAACP wanted to end this inequality. But that wasn't all. The group wanted to show that all segregation was unfair, even if schools had similar resources.

To do this, lawyers planned a series of cases. Black parents tried to send their kids to white schools. When those schools refused, the parents sued.

GONG LUM V. RICE

Many schools also refused to accept Asian Americans. Court cases challenged this, too. One was *Gong Lum v. Rice*. A Chinese man sued a school. It wouldn't let his daughter attend. He said this went against her rights as a US citizen. The Supreme Court disagreed. It said she wasn't white. So, she had to attend another school.

By the 1940s, hundreds of thousands of people across the country were part of the NAACP.

The US Supreme Court is located in Washington, DC.

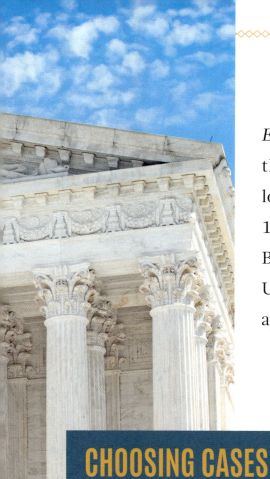

Brown v. Board of Education was one of the NAACP's cases. A lower court heard it in 1951. The parents lost. But they appealed to the US Supreme Court. It agreed to take the case.

CHOOSING CASES

The Supreme Court sometimes hears new cases. But most cases are appeals. People write to the court. They ask it to rethink a lower court's ruling. The Supreme Court gets many appeals each year. It hears only a few. It picks cases it feels are important. The court often selects topics that affect the whole country.

Story Spotlight

THURGOOD MARSHALL

Thurgood Marshall was a lawyer. He worked for the NAACP. He won many important cases. One was against the University of Maryland's law school. Marshall had applied there. But it rejected him. So, he went to Howard University instead. There, he met Charles Hamilton Houston. Houston taught Marshall about using law to make change. They worked on many cases together.

Marshall argued 32 cases at the Supreme Court. He won 29. Later, he joined the Supreme Court. He became its first Black justice.

> Thurgood Marshall served as a Supreme Court justice from 1967 to 1991.

Briggs v. Elliott was one case that was combined with *Brown*. Harry Briggs (above) was one of the parents who sued schools.

Chapter 4
COMBINING CASES

The Supreme Court combined *Brown* with four other cases. All were about segregation in schools. The five cases were similar. Each involved groups of parents. They sued when white schools wouldn't accept their children.

The parents said segregation was unfair. But in each case, the parents lost. So, they decided to appeal. The Supreme Court agreed to rehear the cases.

EARLIER CASES

The NAACP led four of the five cases. Its lawyers said schools were denying kids' rights. In three cases, courts disagreed. In one case, judges partly agreed. They said the schools were unfair to Black students. But they said the problem wasn't segregation. It was that the Black schools weren't as good.

A case is usually heard by a district court first. Then, it can go to a circuit court of appeals. Next, the case may reach the Supreme Court.

Thurgood Marshall (center) talks with other lawyers during arguments about *Brown v. Board*.

The court heard the cases in December 1952. Lawyers for both sides gave evidence. Thurgood Marshall led the NAACP's side. He argued that segregation was always unequal. Marshall used ideas from past cases. He also used studies done by psychologists. He showed how Black students were harmed.

SOCIAL STUDIES

Kenneth and Mamie Clark were psychologists. They researched children. They studied how kids saw themselves. One project showed how segregation made Black kids feel like they were less than other kids. Marshall quoted their work. The Clarks also spoke in court.

After hearing a case, the Supreme Court writes an opinion. It says what the justices think. To make a ruling, more than half must agree.

But for this case, they couldn't agree. Some supported segregation. Some did not. Others were torn. They disliked segregation. But they weren't sure there was a legal reason to end it. So, the court did not decide. Instead, it chose to hear both sides speak again. This move was unusual.

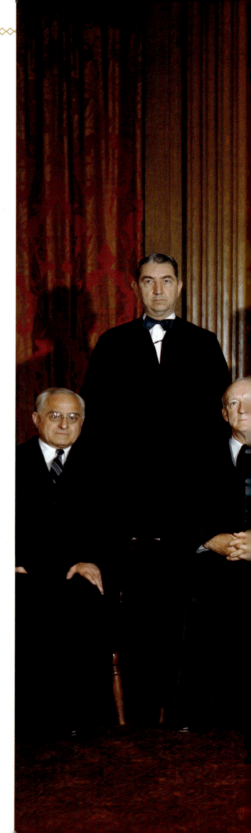

Fred Vinson (bottom center) was the chief justice in 1952.

Story Spotlight

BARBARA ROSE JOHNS

In 1951, Barbara Rose Johns was 16. She went to a segregated high school in Virginia. It didn't have heat or bathrooms. Families asked the school board for improvements. But it ignored them. So, Barbara helped plan a strike. Students left school. They asked for a new building. The NAACP heard about the strike. It started a court case that got combined with *Brown*.

After the walkout, some students faced threats. Barbara moved to Alabama. She later went to college and became a librarian.

Richmond, Virginia, is home to a sculpture honoring Barbara Rose Johns.

Chapter 5
THE SUPREME COURT

The Supreme Court met again in December 1953. By then, it had a new chief justice. Fred Vinson had died. He had not wanted to go against *Plessy*. Earl Warren replaced him.

Chief Justice Warren (bottom center) led a Supreme Court that became known for strengthening civil rights.

The court heard more evidence. On May 17, 1954, it made a decision. This time, all justices agreed. *Plessy* was wrong. Public schools could not be segregated. Chief Justice Warren wrote the court's opinion.

NEW PROOF

At first, justices focused on the Fourteenth Amendment. They asked what the amendment's writers meant by *equal rights*. The justices decided that no one knew. So, they made their own definition. Education was part of equal rights. The justices based this definition on psychology. This was unusual. Courts often relied only on law.

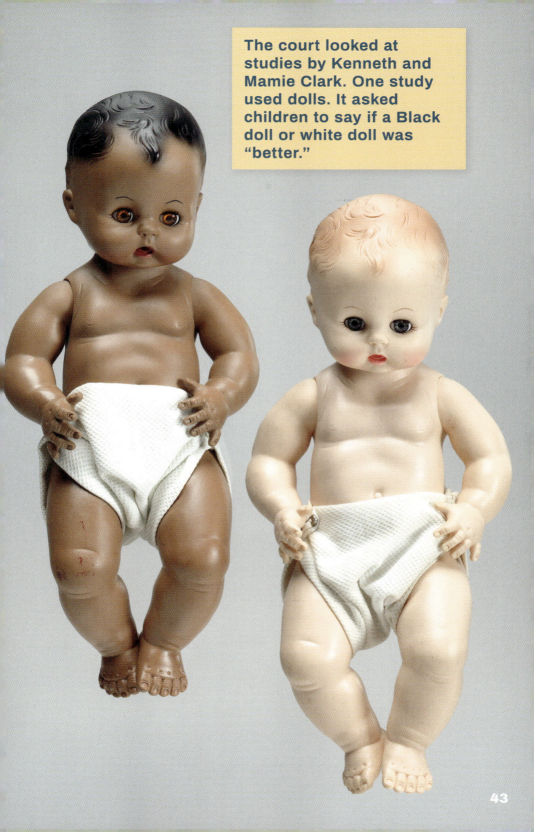

The court looked at studies by Kenneth and Mamie Clark. One study used dolls. It asked children to say if a Black doll or white doll was "better."

The Supreme Court's opinion relied on the Fourteenth Amendment for four of the five cases. This amendment says states cannot limit citizens' rights. The court said segregation limited students' rights.

The fifth case was from Washington, DC. Washington, DC, isn't a state. So, the court used separate reasons to rule against segregation.

THE FIFTH AMENDMENT

The case from Washington, DC, was *Bolling v. Sharpe*. It relied on the Fifth Amendment. That amendment protects people's freedom. Governments may still limit freedom in some ways. But there must be a legal process first. The Supreme Court ruled that segregated schools limited freedom without this process.

James Nabrit Jr. (right) argued the case from Washington, DC. He then helped argue *Brown* at the Supreme Court.

The Supreme Court told schools to integrate. But it didn't say when that had to happen. It also didn't say how. That would be a separate decision.

The court met again in April 1955. On May 31, it gave its opinion. Warren wrote this one, too. He said schools should decide how to integrate. He said they should act quickly. But he didn't set a deadline.

In October 1954, white students at a school in Washington, DC, walked out to protest integration.

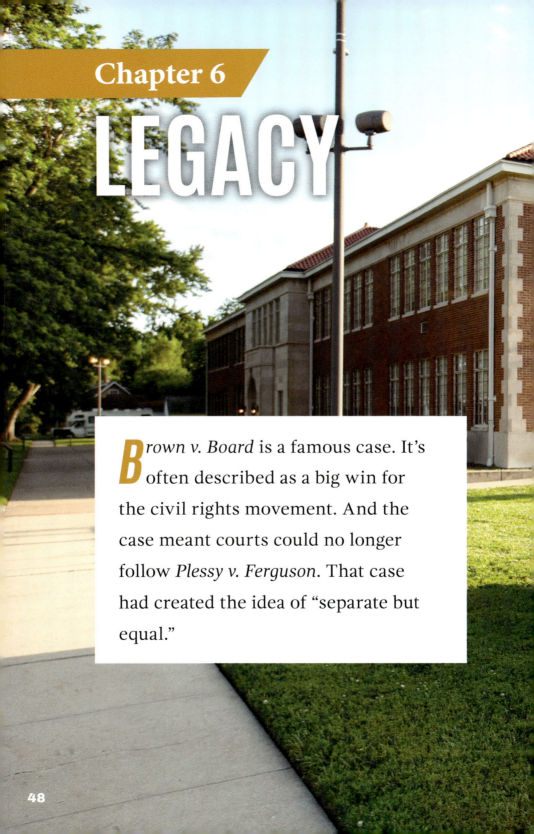

Chapter 6
LEGACY

Brown v. Board is a famous case. It's often described as a big win for the civil rights movement. And the case meant courts could no longer follow Plessy v. Ferguson. That case had created the idea of "separate but equal."

People can visit Monroe Elementary School. That's the all-Black school Linda Brown went to before the court case.

Brown v. Board applied only to public schools. But it set up reasoning that separation was always unequal. This reasoning paved the way for future cases. They helped end segregation in other places, such as stores and buses.

It often took large numbers of people working together to end segregation.

However, change took years. Many states didn't want to integrate. Some white people held protests. They formed mobs outside schools. They tried to keep Black students out. Some of these mobs got violent. They tried to hurt the students.

THE LITTLE ROCK NINE

In 1957, nine Black teenagers tried to attend a white high school in Arkansas. The state's governor opposed integration. He sent state soldiers to stop the students. President Dwight D. Eisenhower responded. He sent US troops to protect the students. But resistance continued. The governor closed all the state's public high schools the next year. The Black students became known as the "Little Rock Nine."

Elizabeth Eckford (right) was one of the Little Rock Nine. She faced racist words from white people as she went to school.

People also found ways to keep students apart. Some parents kept their kids home from school. Some states paid to help white students attend private schools. *Brown* didn't apply to those schools.

By 1960, almost all schools were still segregated. Later laws helped change this. The Civil Rights Act of 1964 said segregated schools could lose funding.

BUSING ORDERS

In the 1970s, courts gave orders about busing. Buses drove students to schools in different areas. That way, schools would have a mix of students.

Busing orders helped Kamala Harris go to an integrated school in the 1970s. She became vice president of the United States in 2021.

Black students did gain more education options. However, problems continued. Many students of color faced racism at their new schools. Access to resources also remained uneven. Students of color were more likely to live in low-income areas. So, their schools often had less money. Activists continued calling for change.

SEGREGATION TODAY

US schools became less segregated in the 1970s and 1980s. That began changing in the 1990s. Courts ended some of the penalties and busing orders. And many schools became segregated based on which families lived nearby.

Many people continue to protest for more equal school conditions.

TIMELINE

1865 — The Thirteenth Amendment to the US Constitution ends slavery.

1868 — The Fourteenth Amendment guarantees equal rights to all citizens.

1896 — The Supreme Court allows segregation in *Plessy v. Ferguson*.

1951 — Black families in Topeka, Kansas, sue in *Brown v. Board of Education*. They lose in a lower court.

1952 — The Supreme Court hears evidence for *Brown* and four other cases about school segregation.

1953 — The Supreme Court meets a second time to hear more evidence.

1954 — The Supreme Court rules on *Brown v. Board of Education*, ending segregation in public schools.

1955 — The Supreme Court meets again and tells schools to act quickly.

1964 — The Civil Rights Act adds penalties for schools that do not integrate.

COMPREHENSION QUESTIONS

Write your answers on a separate piece of paper.

1. Write a paragraph describing the ruling in *Plessy v. Ferguson*.

2. What do you think it means for people to have equal rights?

3. In what year did *Brown v. Board of Education* reach the Supreme Court?
    - A. 1896
    - B. 1950
    - C. 1952

4. What effect did *Brown v. Board of Education* have?
    - A. It ended all segregation right away.
    - B. It helped bring about later changes.
    - C. It didn't make any changes.

5. What does **researched** mean in this book?

*They **researched** children. They studied how kids saw themselves.*

    A. worked to learn about something
    B. worked to change something
    C. worked to get rid of something

6. What does **strike** mean in this book?

*So, Barbara helped plan a **strike**. Students left school. They asked for a new building.*

    A. a time when people stop work or school to call for change
    B. a time when all the schools in a neighborhood close
    C. a time when a court makes a decision about a case

Answer key on page 64.

GLOSSARY

amendments
Changes to the US Constitution.

appealed
Asked to have a case heard again, this time by a higher court.

civil rights movement
The many people who worked together to fight against racism in the United States in the 1950s and 1960s.

Constitution
The document that tells the basic laws and beliefs of the United States.

integrate
To stop dividing people into groups based on race.

precedent
Something used to guide later choices and actions.

psychologists
People who study the mind and how it works.

racism
Hatred or mistreatment of people because of their skin color or ethnicity.

ruled
Made an official decision in a court case.

school board
A group of people who make decisions about public schools.

segregated
Separated based on race, gender, or religion.

TO LEARN MORE

BOOKS

Stratton, Connor. *The Civil Rights Movement.* Mendota Heights, MN: Focus Readers, 2024.

Turner, Myra Faye. *The Little Rock Nine Challenge Segregation: Courageous Kids of the Civil Rights Movement.* North Mankato, MN: Capstone Press, 2023.

Weston, Margeaux. *Brown v. Board of Education: A Day That Changed America.* North Mankato, MN: Capstone Press, 2022.

ONLINE RESOURCES

Visit **www.apexeditions.com** to find links and resources related to this title.

ABOUT THE AUTHOR

Brienna Rossiter is a writer and editor who lives in Minnesota.

INDEX

amendments, 11, 16, 42, 44
Arkansas, 52

Bolling v. Sharpe, 44
Brown, Linda, 4, 7
Brown, Oliver, 4, 7
Brown v. Board of Education, 7, 27, 31, 38, 48, 50, 54

Civil Rights Act of 1875, 11
Civil Rights Act of 1964, 54

Eisenhower, Dwight D., 52

Gong Lum v. Rice, 24

Harlan, John Marshall, 16

integration, 46, 52

Jim Crow laws, 13–14, 18
Johns, Barbara Rose, 38

Kansas, 4, 7

Little Rock Nine, 52

Marshall, Thurgood, 28, 35

National Association for the Advancement of Colored People (NAACP), 18, 21, 23–24, 27, 28, 32, 35, 38

Plessy, Homer, 14, 16
Plessy v. Ferguson, 14, 16, 21, 40, 42, 48
psychology, 35, 42

Reconstruction, 13

slavery, 8, 11
South Carolina, 23

US Civil War, 8, 13
US Constitution, 11

Vinson, Fred, 40
Virginia, 38

Warren, Earl, 40, 42, 46
Washington, DC, 44

ANSWER KEY:
1. Answers will vary; 2. Answers will vary; 3. C; 4. B; 5. A; 6. A